TUESDAY TAKES ME THERE

The Healing Journey of a Veteran and his Service Dog

★ ★ ★

Fmr. Captain **LUIS CARLOS MONTALVÁN**, *USA*
with **BRET WITTER** ★ *photos by* **DAN DION**

POST HILL PRESS

A POST HILL PRESS BOOK
ISBN: 978-1-68261-106-7
ISBN (eBook): 978-1-68261-107-4

TUESDAY TAKES ME THERE
The Healing Journey of a Veteran and his Service Dog
© 2016 by Luis Carlos Montalván with Bret Witter
All Rights Reserved

Cover Photograph by Dan Dion
Cover Design by Quincy Alivio
Interior design by Neuwirth & Associates

Post Hill
PRESS

Post Hill Press
275 Madison Avenue, 14th Floor
New York, NY 10016
posthillpress.com

Printed in Canada

This morning, like every morning, my friend Luis wakes up to this.

Rise and shine! It's a traveling day!

We have to say good-bye to Mike, who let us stay with him last night.

Like Luis, Mike is a military veteran. They both fought in the Iraq War. In war, Luis saw and felt a lot of pain. That caused a condition called PTSD. It was hard for Luis to live a normal life with PTSD, so he was matched with me: Tuesday. I'm a service dog.

Luis is better now, but it's still hard for him to deal with strange places and crowds. So when we travel, we try to stay with friends like Mike, because they understand us, and we love them. Veterans are our family.

Staying with Mike was great. But, it's time to go. We have some place to be tonight! So I give Mike a hug. And then, Luis and I are off on a journey . . .

. . . walking on our own six feet. (Or seven, if you count Luis's cane.)

"No need to hurry, Tuesday!" Luis says, as I walk exactly beside him to help him balance. "We're taking the ferry."

Awesome!

What's a ferry?

Luis laughs. "That big orange boat is a ferry. Can you see it? The Staten Island Ferry travels between Staten Island and Manhattan."

STATEN ISLAND is one of the five boroughs (towns) that together make New York City.

A ferry boat?

A ferry boat!

Look at all these other boats.

A tourist boat.

A Coast Guard boat.

A tug boat.

A fire boat.

And a statue, too. She's beautiful.

What's her name?

THE STATUE OF LIBERTY was a gift of friendship from France to the United States in 1886.

"Look Tuesday, it's Manhattan."

So many tall buildings, a few small buildings, and one that's taller than them all.
Let's go there!

The bus is soooo slow . . .

Come on . . .   come on . . .

Wow. That's the tallest building I have ever seen! It's 94 floors tall.

Luis touches the names on the wall in front of me. It's a memorial wall, with a pool of water in the middle. "Triumph can grow from tragedy," Luis says.

Then he smiles. "You want to see it from another view?"

FREEDOM TOWER stands near the September 11th Memorial on ground that was part of the World Trade Center. It is the sixth tallest building in the world.

Lift off!

Dog in a helicopter! Dog in a helicopter! And there it is, Freedom Tower!

"It is a beacon of hope," Luis says.

There's Lady Liberty, too!

Let's see:

   Helicopter. Boat. BUS. *Feet*.

   Sky. WATER. *Paws*. Street.

How else can we travel? HOW ABOUT . . .

Underground!

A subway is a train that runs underground. This one takes us through a tunnel. Stay calm, Luis. I'm always here for you. And there's love at the end of this ride.

See, I told you.

 LOVE (sculpture), by Robert Indiana, on 54th Street in Manhattan, is one of the most photographed sites in New York City.

Now on to Central Park, where we meet a carriage horse named Bruno.
Can we ride with him?

Of course we can!

Thanks, Bruno, from one hard working animal to another.

We've traveled so many ways so far. BOAT, *bus*, horse, *helicopter* and a SUBWAY CAR.

But, we still haven't left New York City!

And, it's so crowded. Now Luis *really* needs me. His PTSD makes him nervous around strangers, so when we're on a busy street, I stay in front to clear the way.

We made it!
High paws!

 PENN STATION is the busiest transport center in the United States. It serves more than 600,000 travelers a day. That's more than 213 million a year.

As we walk down the stairs, Luis holds the handle on my harness.
It helps to keep him steady. While on our journey, I'm always ready.

Make way,
service dog
coming
through!

We find our seat on the Amtrak train. Luis makes a comfy place for me. I did a good job taking care of him, so he takes care of me. It's his way of showing he loves me.

I put my paw on his foot to tell him I love him too.

Are we there yet?

Are we there yet?

We're here! But, where is here?

"We're at Union Station, the main train station in Washington, D.C., Tuesday. Do you want to visit a friend?"

Yeah!

 In 1903, PRESIDENT THEODORE ROOSEVELT signed an act "to provide a union railroad station in the District of Columbia." Union Station opened in 1907.

We walk to the
United States
Capitol building.

We visit Senator Al Franken. In 2009, we met Al when Luis and I helped him and Senator Johnny Isakson pass a law to partner more service dogs with veterans.

Thanks, Al! I love you, too.

But, we can't stay. We have a lot to see and do . . .

By our six feet . . .

. . . and by pedicab.
(It's a "pedaling taxi cab!")

Wow, that's a cool building.

 THE WASHINGTON MONUMENT is both the world's tallest stone structure and the world's tallest obelisk, standing 554 feet 7 1/32 inches tall.

Then we travel by
wooden horse . . .
or is it by dragon?

Hey man, this
thing keeps going
round and round!

Okay, you're right. Let's rest.

It's been a busy day. We've traveled by boat, bus, Bruno, and merry-go-round. By subway, helicopter, pedal-man, and train. We've walked for miles. We're still not there.

What's left to take?

Airplanes! Airplanes! Giant airplanes!
(Can you see us? We're so small.)

There's even a spaceship that landed on the moon.

Commander Tuesday to Ground Control.

Come in Ground Control!

 THE SMITHSONIAN NATIONAL AIR AND SPACE MUSEUM holds the largest collection of historic aircraft and spacecraft in the world including the Wright Flyer, the first airplane. The Wright Brothers flew it 120 feet in 1903.

It's getting late. The mission waits. But Luis wants to make an important stop, so we take a double-decker bus . . .

 THE JEFFERSON MEMORIAL honors Thomas Jefferson. He wrote the Declaration of Independence and was also the third U.S. President.

ARLINGTON NATIONAL CEMETERY is the nation's honored resting place for veterans. The first burial took place on May 13, 1864, during the Civil War.

. . . to a famous cemetery. We want to pay respect to those who served and died in war. Some died in Iraq, where Luis was wounded. Some died two hundred years ago. But they are all veterans, so they are our pack. That's dog-speak for family.

Praying with Luis, I feel his heart and share what's inside: sadness, honor, love and pride.

Now it's time for one last ride.

A red convertible! I wish I could drive.

We cross a bridge into the countryside. We're in a hurry, but there's always time . . .

 LOYS STATION COVERED BRIDGE in Thurmont, Maryland, was built in 1848. Covered Bridges were designed to protect the wooden structures from the weather.

. . . to tromp *through* **the flowers . . .**

. . . and *splash* in the water . . .

. . . *and* . . .

Oh wait! The mission! I almost forgot.

There's a reason we took
a bus,
a boat,
a car,
a train,
a horse,
a pedaling man,
a double decker bus,
a merry-go-round,
a subway, a helicopter,
an-almost-airplane,
a rocket-in-my-dreams,
and our own six feet.

It's the most important reason of all, because
we're going to the most important place of all . . .

A local library,
where we see
the smiling faces
of friends like you.